Heaven
24/7
Living in the Light

Kathryn Jones

M. Celeste Martin
x

Books by Kathryn Elizabeth Jones

A River of Stones

Parable Series

Conquering Your Goliaths: A Parable of the Five Stones

Conquering Your Goliaths: Guidebook

The Feast: A Parable of the Ring

The Gift: A Parable of the Key

The Parables of Virginia Bean

Heaven 24/7

Living in the Light
With M. Celeste Martin

Marketing Your Book on a Budget

Susan Cramer Mysteries

Scrambled

Sunny Side-Up

Hard Boiled

Heaven 24/7

Living in the Light

Kathryn Elizabeth Jones
M. Celeste Martin

Idea Creations Press
www.ideacreationspress.com

ISBN-13: 9780996665759
ISBN-10: 0996665757

Library of Congress Control Number: 2016937205

Printed in the U.S.A.

I love it. Very open experiences to help people know they are not the only ones experiencing tough issues. I love your insights and the "parables" you open each section with and reference in the chapter.

I once had a dream/personal revelation where I spoke with Christ at a turning point in my life where I had to make a serious decision about what direction I wanted to go. I felt that powerful, overwhelming love that fills your whole body you spoke of; a level of love that really is hard to fathom in our earthly existence. I must say, more than once - especially during tough times - I have remembered that feeling to have it lift me and I can't wait to return to my Heavenly Father and Savior to feel it all the time. It is truly an amazing feeling.

- Debby Martin

Acknowledgments

We could not have written and published this book without the loving support of many.

A big thank you to Valerie Tomer and Debby Martin.
To our support crew (families):

Chris Martin, Aaron Martin and Chelsea Martin and all those who allowed us to use their stories, but asked to remain anonymous.

We'd also like to thank Chelsea Martin and Jason Cox for their help with the cover photo and Douglas Jones for his endless support in finalizing the cover photo, the formatting as well as the business site.

THANK YOU!

Before you Begin

We invite you to take a few moments at the end of each chapter with questions and write down your thoughts, memories and inspiration about the chapter to help you in your learning process.

Beginnings

Beginnings

It happened on an ordinary Thursday, made extra-ordinary by two people who sat across from one another at the local Village Inn. It was their day to talk.

One friend was a mere 59 years, the other, just grasping her early 50s (she was 53). In each of their individual lives they had come to know God, had heard his voice, had listened to his direction, and today, on a simply ordinary day, had come to share.

In reality, any day when these two friends got together the day could never be seen as ordinary, it just wasn't possible. What always occurred was something extra-ordinary, something heavenly, something life changing.

And today wasn't going to be any different.

Today, the two friends shared, and during the sharing the 53 year old said, "It's too bad we can't live in heaven 24/7."

"That's a great idea for your next book," offered the 59 year old. "I mean, you could go anywhere with it. Talk about your journey. Write about what it would mean to live a heavenly life; to see what was real and what was an illusion."

The 53 year old blinked and reached for her notebook (a notebook for gathering facts; a notebook that had been scribbled on by her 5 year old grand-daughter). She felt a piece of heaven enter her soul as she searched for a blank page and wrote:

Heaven 24/7.

Kathryn

It's too bad we can't live in heaven 24/7.

But what if we could tap into heaven whenever we wanted to, grab a handful of blue sky, reach for a rainbow, scatter the feelings of love born there whenever we needed it or wanted it?

What if a girl could fly? Where would she travel first?

What if a hippo could talk? And we actually learned something from him?

What if a dragon could not only fly, but sing? Would we listen?

What if we could reach heaven 24/7?

Right now, in this very second, as you read that very last line, did you think to yourself, *"How can I truly reach heaven while I'm still planted firmly on this earth?"*

How truly?

Celeste

I have felt, even known that the concept of *living Heaven 24/7* is a reality, though living this kind of life is often unrecognized in my daily, busy, hustle and bustle life.

Stuck, yep, I've been stuck many a time. I've thought, "Why am I having such a miserable experience?" I have thought the proverbial, "Why me?" on many occasions. Yet, I have learned the beauty of this:

What if *each moment* is shaped, sculpted per se, given by heavenly design *just for me*? Just for me to…look at it…make a choice…hear or see something vital, critical, or beautiful…be inspired…be chastened…be in the right place to serve someone or be an instrument to answer their plea or prayer? What if?

What if *this* very moment is given to look to heaven, for heaven is always waiting for me to embrace it. Am I paying attention? When I reach for Heaven, Heaven always reaches back. Am I keeping myself connected to what already is tangibly here on this earth and available to me…Heaven? Hummmm…

Glimpses

Glimpses

In every life, even in this one, there are glimpses, moments when the veil is parted, and for a moment, maybe even a day or a week, heaven is open to our view.

In preparing this book Celeste and I wanted to share some of our glimpses; quick reminders if you will, moments of divine intervention or reflection given to us by the greatest light of all. These glimpses have brought us closer to God, closer to who He is, who we are, and who He wants us to become.

For where there is light there is truth. And where there is truth there are stories.

What are yours?

Within this book is opportunity for you to see, to expand your mind and your heart, to know yourself and to know your Savior better.

Will you take on the heavenly challenge?

Celeste and I would like to share a few stories of our own, because it is through the events and stories of our lives that we have come to recognize the evidence that we live connected to heaven 24/7 amidst eternity.

17

Stories

Stories

What are your Stories?
You have them, you know

Celeste

Stories. I love hearing and learning from stories told by others. Many a time I have been given an answer, directed to a book, song, article, place, etc., through someone's story that touched me. We all have stories. Some funny, some tragic, some whimsical, some just mundane, and then some absolute gifts. Concrete evidences that I live, nestled among the eternities.

A few years ago, before moving to Utah, and while living on the Oregon coast, I had been attending a training here in the Salt Lake area. Sunday morning after the training I boarded my flight to return to Oregon. The flight was peaceful and beautiful as usual. The flight path approaching the Portland airport would take us in a sweeping semi-circle ever so close to majestic Mt. Hood.

As we began that sweep, I found myself strangely drawn to Mt. Hood's majesty. And then it began…the music. The most glorious, heavenly music, undeniably offering praises, and coming…from the mountain! Yes!

And no, I'm not delusional. The earth, Mt. Hood, was singing in glorious praises of its creator…and I knew it.

The experience was absolutely indescribable. I cried. The music filled every fiber of me. It was so glorious. There aren't words to describe it. There truly aren't. The scripture of 'all things' bearing witness (Alma 30:44), all things…literally came to pass for me in that moment.

As I breathed, the earth breathed; as I looked up, the earth looked upward and there was a great sense of 'oneness' with all things - connected to heaven. Awestriking!

Yet another time:

We were on a trip back to Salt Lake from Oregon, north of Saint George in our jeep. It was late at night. My husband, Chris, was sleeping in the passenger seat, the kids were asleep in the back. The gas light had been on for several miles; I knew we would be out of gas shortly. I also knew there were many miles ahead before I was going to be able to get some gas, enough miles ahead that I became concerned.

The coolest thing happened! All of a sudden everything got really quiet and calm, and the breeze…suddenly the jeep was lifted onto that breeze, and I'm telling you, we were carried on that breeze to the gas station that was many miles beyond the gas tank's capacity. There was no reason for us to not run out of gas. The calm, silent sound of that heavenly breeze was so prominent, there was no denying that we were being carried.

I'll never forget that experience.

Think of the miraculous events when the Savior was on the earth. How many fishes did he have? How many loaves did he have? How many people did he feed?

These are real things that happened. No fantasy. And it's awesome. Heaven is active in our lives every day.

Kathryn

When we moved from California we were out of money. We were all in the moving van. Our car wasn't road worthy enough, so it was being towed by our moving van. My husband and I and our three kids were in the front seat of the moving van like sardines in a can.

The gas tank was full, but as we traveled, I watched the gage dwindle down to red. Reaching Salt Lake City, we were still moving, and the gas tank was empty. We had no money to get gas, but we somehow made it to my mom's front door.

One more:

I was going to work in my old, old car. We'd managed to save $350 to buy it to get me to and from work. You could see the road through the floor boards.

I thought, "I just gotta do this. I've got to get to work and this is all I can afford."

I got to work and I sat in that parking lot so sorry about having to drive an old, worn out car, when all of a sudden I heard the heavens open and I heard music. I sat in that old clunker and heard the angels sing.

I might have been in this old clunker of a car but I knew I wasn't far away from heaven. Separated by a veil, yes, but I knew I wasn't alone.

And this is Heaven 24/7. But not all of it.

A Stone

A Stone

Do you carry one stone or two?

Imagine that you are at a great lake, and that on this lake are beauties to behold. Large aspens, yellow and purple wildflowers; the best and most refreshing breeze possible is caressing your face.

You are not alone at this lake. You are standing by the water, looking out into the distance, feeling the breeze, smelling the mountain air. It feels like heaven.

Someone is suddenly beside you.

You don't look at him at first, it's almost as if you *can't* look, but you feel him there and you know he is looking out at the lake as you are.

That's when you first notice the rock.

The rock is smooth and fits within the palm of your hand. It is black. It is dark. It feels heavier than it should.

"I can take the rock if you'd like me to," says God. "You just need to hand it to me."

But you don't know if you can. You are thinking about the pain your sister caused you just last week; the moment your husband confessed the lie, the time your mother forgot you.

"Can't I just throw it into the water?" you ask.

"No," says God.

"I feel like hitting her with it," you say.

"I know," says God.

"I don't know if I can let go of it."

"I am here," says God, "when you're ready."

We all carry stones. No, I'm not talking about gallstones, or kidney stones (though we may have the unpleasant misfortune of traveling there for a time). We might even be carrying milestones, especially if we're one of those people who likes to take stock of where we are in our life and where we're heading, but these stones, if you'll pardon the *fun*, are stones we carry inside ourselves that no doctor can see, no foot can kick or remove or throw.

They can only be removed by God.

Celeste

My mom was a smoker. I was taught and raised with strong health guidelines and I remember the day my mom discovered that I was smoking. She was furious at me.

I asked, "Who taught me? You taught me" (Mom was a smoker at the time).

And so I went through my teen years. I got to the point in my life where I'd become inactive in my church and living a very worldly life. I smoked and drank. It's important for people to know, you're going to make some really dumb mistakes when you're living that lifestyle.

But, there's a way back; you don't have to stay there. So I made a choice, based on a series of events at that time in my life, that it was time to stop smoking, drinking, and living in the world.

As a child, I'd been taught truth through the Gospel of Jesus Christ, and I wanted to turn my life around-give back the 'stones'. I wanted my life back with Heavenly Father and the Savior. I wanted my life back in order. I had the *desire* to be back with my Heavenly Father and the Savior. With that *chosen* decision, I gave back the stones of smoking and drinking.

And then came another gift of divine intervention, a 'tender mercy' if you will. My brother invited me to fly to Europe, Germany, to stay with his family and help out with the children, and I said, "Send me the ticket."

But I had another stone, well really a boulder. This one, a humongous mountain of boulders; a lover. To give away this boulder I couldn't just move to the next town. I had to go 6,000 miles away.

So I left the boulder. I was truly on a flight to Germany to change my life. Yes, I partied the whole way. It's a journey remember. I smoked and drank the whole way, partying with some very marvelous yet worldly people, stepped off the plane and never touched another cigarette or another sip of alcohol.

The truly marvelous and miraculous thing about that? I never had a craving for either after that point! My heart had turned. I was on that flight for many reasons and I had already made the choice, the decision to allow Heavenly Father and the Savior back into my life. Both of them knew there was still that little part of me that had to party, but they also knew that I had made my decision and my choice was them. I fully believe that this change of heart was nothing less than a gift given to me because of my true desires, and I had chosen *Them*. I never craved again EVER.

I so desire for people to realize that they can have their lives and have their hearts turned like that. It will be a process but it can happen for them, for you; in a heartbeat. There are stories about prophets being so horrible, wicked, and then turning and becoming so righteous. You don't have to be a prophet for this to happen! It happened for me…it can happen for you.

So, back to the boulder…leaving the lover.

Keep in mind that I have recommitted to my Heavenly Father and the Savior. So I have to give him up. This is not a stone, this is a mountain of boulders. So on the flight to Germany I'm not only giving up smoking and drinking, I'm giving up my lover. I'm giving it all. I have to. I have to do my part on that plane.

I've accepted the ticket. I have embraced the *desires* of my heart (which gave me great courage by the way). I have made the promise. I have told the Lord, "I will go wherever you need me to go. I can safely give you the boulders, knowing that the boulders aren't going to come back. These are huge and in my heart, but I can't have them anymore."

One day, not too long after arriving in Germany, my sister-in-law and I are working in the kitchen and the phone rings. It's my lover. My sister-in-law is petrified that I'll be persuaded to return to him. I'm not and I don't.

I love him, but I don't want to return to him. My *choice* is to love God more.

To this day it is interesting to me how I got to solidify that conviction, that conversion, through a series of opposition that required me to re-make, or stick to the commitment. I could have chosen differently at any moment. The true desires of my heart were strong and I could not deny them.

About a month later, while still in Germany, and at a church single adult function, I meet a young 21-year-old guy climbing around on rocks (funny I just realized they were boulders) like a kid. I only say that because I'm 27 and he's 21. I'm a mature, seasoned woman. He's a young, handsome E-4. Here enters Chris into my life.

Chris sees me. In his words he's thinking, "I'd better get off these rocks."

He sees me and he knows. We walk toward each other and instantly the spirit says, "This is going to be your husband."

I reply, "*Really?*" But I knew, and I knew that Heavenly Father was guiding me and that I needed to be paying attention. I desired for my life to be in alignment with His laws and His will.

They say hindsight is wonderful, true enough. I can look back and see the entire process; Heaven 24/7. This was an amazing period of time in my life when so much strength was created within me. I'd always had a testimony. I knew the Church was truly re-organized on the earth and that it was true. But there is a difference between testimony and conversion. I had a testimony, and that was critical. But I wasn't converted to Heavenly Father and the Savior until I'd made the choice to make *Them* the very focus of my life. And because of that testimony, formed in my childhood years, my conversion was able to take hold.

What are you desiring?

If you're desiring to hold onto your stones, whatever they may be, if you would rather keep them, He'll let you. I still have some of my own but am better at letting them go. Desire and choice are two of the keys.

I know that beyond this life there is something so glorious that I can't even get my brain wrapped around it. So, these periods of what can seem like hell on earth, they're my proving ground, they're *your* proving ground.

I get to do my best which is often so pitiful. But it's the best I can do at the time. That's when Christ comes in and says, "Here, let me show you." I've had divine intervention, tender mercy's as the scriptures call them, many a time. And because of this I know that Heavenly Father is involved in my life every second and has a grander design for me.

That's why the Savior says, "Come unto me. Follow me. Let me show you."

Kathryn

Stones. We all have them. They might all be pebbles, but I doubt it. Some of the stuff we carry are of the bigger variety, the ones that weigh heavily across our backs.

Such was the case with me.

I had been hurt plenty of times in my life, but this time, someone had hurt my husband. The stone on my back was as thick, as heavy as a house. Except I wasn't in a house, I was at the courthouse. And the person in front of me, standing before the judge, was the man that had physically hurt my husband and had been put in jail because of it.

My husband had instantly forgiven him.

But I couldn't. My husband might have died.

I'd prayed. Hard. Over and over and over. "Take away this pain." "Help me!" "Help me to forgive him!" "I can't carry this!" "Please!"

But I couldn't do it. I carried the stone for days, going over and over the pain I felt. As my husband healed, I'd review the episode over and over in my brain. I was literally making myself sick.

Finally the day came. The morning of the proceedings. I walked into the courthouse though I didn't know how I was going to face the man who had hurt my husband, but I knew my husband had let it go. It made me angry that he had let it go. Didn't the man deserve jail time? It was his first time in jail but so what? He might have killed my husband!

Still feeling the turmoil of hate and pain I walked out to the second floor from the elevator, my husband beside me. The man was standing about twenty feet from me. I could barely breathe. I prayed again. And then it happened. Something like a calm wave caressed my heart and stayed there. And then, as if it had always existed, I felt such great love; a love I'd never felt before for this person who had injured my husband. God loved him!

Could I do any less?

I hardly know how I reached him, but suddenly I was embracing him. And the rock, the huge boulder was gone.

There was another individual a part of this scenario, who I chose not to forgive that day. Years have gone by, and as the years have passed, I often thought about what I might have done differently. But there were just too many broken promises, too many times I felt she owed me an apology, too many times that she'd hurt my daughter over her not so plain and simple - fear.

I just couldn't do it then, and seven years later, I still couldn't do it.

Still, I'd carried the boulder for quite some time, the anger breathing within my soul like a constantly heated hot plate. Was it finally time to let this stone go?

You may think it funny that I could forgive one person on that day I was in court, but not another, and I suppose it sounds funny when you think of all the time I've wasted hating her. But then again, the Lord is patient isn't he? He wants me to truly work through this issue, and if it takes me seven years, so be it. When it is done, it will be done forevermore.

I began to heal from this wound just a few days ago as I watched an old *Highway to Heaven* episode. Here was a man, a Nazi believer, who had a perfectly good heart - at least physically speaking, and a less-than-physically-perfect Jew, in need of a heart transplant. They are both at the hospital at the same time. The Nazi, kept alive by a machine - his son has accidently shot him, is brain dead, and a Jew in need of a new heart so he might continue to live his life is in his own hospital bed. Only he doesn't want the Nazi's heart - especially from the man who murdered his son.

You can see the huge dilemma.

A heart, but not just any heart, has been given to a man who needs it. What does the Jewish man do? He screams. He is angry. He doesn't want to live. How can he, with such a heart beating inside his body?

But then, looking up from his hospital bed he sees his parents - killed during the holocaust. He sees his son, killed recently at the hands of the Nazi whose wife has gifted his heart. His family says, "Don't give up. You can't give up. You must continue. If you give up, evil will win."

The Jewish man knows he must live. For the first time he sees his new heart for what it is - a gift from God.

And suddenly, I see it. The evening in the emergency room when I first began to hate her. I see my husband, blood drying on his t-shirt, the marks of stabbing in various places on his head. And I see her. She is apologizing for her loved one, as if he is incapable of doing it himself. She is apologizing and reaching for me to embrace her.

And that's when it began.

Some gifts are heavy. But it is our perception of them that creates the heaviness, not the gift itself. The truth is, I couldn't forgive her then. I had to go to court, take care of the first heaviness, and then allow the working of years - perhaps even this movie - to finally allow me to see the truth.

I will never be able to change her. All I can do is change my heart.

- Do you have any boulders in your life that you'd like to get rid of?
- Do you believe Christ can relieve you of this burden?
- Are you ready and willing to remove the layers of pain?
- How will you remove the pain? What steps will you take?
- Do you truly believe Christ can remove all stones and boulders from your life?
- Are you ready to see the truth?

Eyeglasses

Eyeglasses

How well do you see?

Imagine that you're at a science fair, and, according to the instructions of your teacher, required to put together a project. You're not sure what to do; it could be a volcano, a water project, something to do with electricity or why your cat is always coughing up fur balls. It really doesn't matter to you, you only know this instruction must be followed; if not, no grade.

The time comes, and with your project chosen, you stand in the hallway waiting somewhat impatiently for the doors to open.

Why won't they open?

Your eyeglasses are dark, it's hard to see in the dimly lit hall. To make matters worse, you can barely see through the left side of your glasses; the surface of the glass is dark. The right side, blocked by some imaginary black line, does not allow you to even see out.

The door opens.

You see the tables and chairs made ready. But barely. Everything is blank, empty, waiting to be filled.

The noise increases as you enter the room. But it is hard to see. Everything is so hard to see.

We all think we see clearly, even with a new pair of glasses, contacts, or even, dare I say it, laser surgery. But what is reality? How much do we truly see?

1 Corinthians 13:12 says, *For now we see through a glass, darkly; but then face to face: now I know in part; but then shall I know even as also I am known.*

What does that verse mean to you, exactly?

Is it speaking about how we truly see in this mortal life; darkly, or at least darker than we could? And what would it feel like, look like to see the Savior "face to face"? We have the faith that He is there, and that He is real, but later, (how much later we know not) "we shall...know".

What does it feel like, look like to "know even as also [you] are known"?

Think about that for a moment.

Who knows you without any hesitation, without any doubt as to who you are and what you can accomplish? Who knows your quirks, your favorite sins, what you do with your time when no one is watching, but Him?

I truly believe that in that day, in that moment, when we truly see ourselves for who we are, we will also see Him.

Right now we have some sort of beam in our eye, blocking not only our individual potential but the living, breathing potential of everyone else on this planet.

Think about it.

When was the last time you complained about your weight, your lack of patience, your mother? When was the last time you gossiped about your next door neighbor; the one who always forgets to mow his/her lawn, or the church member who always forgets your name, or complains about the way you do things?

When was the last time the mote in your eye was so large, so mammoth, so eye-splintering deep, there was no room for the light to penetrate from either side?

Either you couldn't see out, or someone else couldn't see *in*?

Seeing through a "glass darkly" is part of the mortal experience; so is acknowledging the "beam" in our own eye.

But to see, truly see, one must trust in the eyes of the Master who sees all.

Kathryn

When I was seven, my parents divorced and my mother re-married. Along with the adjustments of a new father, I had three new siblings that I was supposed to get along with.

And I appeared to get along with them, at least outwardly. But inside I was angry at my father who had left me, and angry at my new siblings who'd taken away the close-knit feelings of security that I had once had with my mother by demanding so much of her time.

I might have yelled at everyone, run away, started into drugs and escaped into alcohol, but I did none of those things.

Perhaps I took the cowards way out, but more than likely I did what only a quiet, seven-year-old who's lost a parent, while gaining new siblings, could do.

I hid.

It was simply easier to escape into silence, gather inside my room with my books and belongings, than face anyone ever again who might leave me.

And that's what I did for many years. And I thought I was happy.

I saw myself as a shy girl who preferred the constancy of books for company, and I was happy to spend my entire life that way.

But you know how the Lord is.

Fortunately, he was able to see things a bit more clearly than I was. He was able to see who I needed and at what times I needed them. A friend, one good friend, who would listen. A new father in my life who would care for me as much as his own child. A young man who would prove his interest in me even through my shyness and awkwardness.

I would almost marry another, but then came strong parents who knew something I had simply misplaced. They knew of my potential, and counseled me to wait.

When Doug came into my life it was easy to love him. He was confident; a trait I lacked, and saw beauty in me (still does) even when my glasses are the darkest.

But my life after marriage was not perfect.

As the years went on, there were struggles. Many struggles. And there came a day when I wondered if I could really love him again. I wondered if things would ever be the same. He'd broken my heart.

We were in the temple. I'd just come out into the foyer, and as I walked out I looked towards the men's dressing room. Doug was just leaving; coming in my direction. I watched as he came up to me all in white. And in that moment, that instant of Heaven 24/7, I did not see him as he is today, I saw him as he is going to be.

And he was glorious.

That thought, that glimpse, comes to me often now when times get hard, when I don't think I can make it. I see him there, all dressed in white and glowing with love. My glimpse into eternity.

Celeste

I was sexually abused by numerous loved ones in my life. A circumstance too many have faced. This particular (loved one) for years molested me as a child and into my teens.

Now that I'm older, people have asked me, *"Why didn't you say something? Why did you allow it to happen?"* (Blame is typically a beam by the way).

"Because I loved him" is my response. I did not understand the ugliness nor the gravity of the circumstance. What I knew at the time was he was an awesome, funny little man that wasn't anyone significant, but, oh my gosh, he brought so much fun into my life. He loved to play cards. We would play for hours and hours.

Now some people might look at that and say, *"Well, he was manipulating you."*

Well, I don't know. Looking back at it, I don't believe he was manipulating me. This is what I do know. When he became deathly ill and in the hospital on his deathbed, (I'm older at this time), I visited him for the last time. I remember how he cried and cried and cried over the shame of his erring way, and in that moment I SAW him.

I saw someone with an illness, with a disease, one that he probably didn't understand fully himself nor understand how to overcome. In that moment I was so sorry for him. How could I keep the enormously ugly, painful, uncomfortable things that sexual abuse can bring within me? None of that ugliness mattered at that moment because I *saw* him.

I vividly recall the tender thought, *"Oh, you dear one. You're going to get to pay the price,"* entering my mind and heart. I knew I was not the one he ultimately would face. I felt the depth of his tears as he faced me. I could not imagine the depths he would feel as he faced the Savior.

But I also loved him so much. I wanted to let him know that I loved him, and that I understood, and for me, not that what he did was okay or acceptable, but I just wanted him to know that I would be okay and I understood.

I understand why many people may avoid this subject. There are many in my life that have faced these types of trials and evils. I do understand. Yet, I know that holding on to the stones and boulders; continuing to see only through dark, dim glasses does not allow for and give place to the atonement of Christ in your life!

Let God be the judge.

Does that mean that what happened is all hunky dory? Of course not. Does that mean that life can be filled with so much more joy because you've gotten past the pain? Yes! Have you learned about the atonement? Have you learned to give the pain back to God and the Savior? Are your eyeglasses still dark?

- How much do you truly see?
- How easy is it to judge what you don't truly see?
- When have you judged?
- What have you done with this judgment?

The Path

The Path

What path do you travel?

Imagine you are in a cave. The cave is dark, cold and cramped. Many people, both young and old surround you. You can't see more than their forms, and the bench you are sitting on is being shared by others. You have no real space.

Suddenly, a man arrives. He is dressed in white. He takes your hand. You follow him out.

Outside the cave there is a long and winding path. From your vantage point you can see that you are somewhere below the large mountain, and the path is filled with rocks and weeds. You can also see that there is a house just a few feet from where you are standing; also, a nice flowing river to the right.

You choose the house.

At the door you look around. There is no one there, only you and the house and all that lies inside it. You go in. You surround yourself with stuff. Big stuff, small stuff, stuff that takes your breath away.

You like your stuff, but one day you leave the house and return to the path.

God is waiting.

He takes your hand.

You travel up the path. You walk by the water. You travel up the mountain.

This is life.

You fall. You get sick. You're carried up the mountain.

Finally, you swim. A cleansing has occurred. But in time you forget, and one day you're once again at the foot of the mountain.

You see the house.

Life isn't always easy to traverse. There are those noxious weeds. But they must be there along with the flowers. We wouldn't grow if nothing graced our path but colorful wildflowers. In the same breath we wouldn't grow if all we managed to find on the path of our life was rocks and weeds.

In every facet of life, whether in the dark cave, inside a beautifully decorated house, or walking the path called life, God is always waiting to take us up the path, a path where the water is always plentiful and never ceases.

But we have a choice to make. We can choose the dark cave where we see little. We can choose the house of learning and sometimes, distraction. Or we can choose the path and walk with God.

Celeste

I've learned a lot in my own house, the house of my life. This is when I try to figure things out on my own. It's tough sometimes in that house. And sometimes after talking with the Lord, hand in hand, I go back to that house.

Woe is me, and my life is so pitiful! I have to get out of my stuff, get out of my house because there's a path. A path!

It's one thing to be in darkness; you don't want to live there, but a house with a toilet, a kitchen, all of the conveniences; this is comfortable.

How many have wanted to leave their spouse? How many have had those dark thoughts?

Just this last year alone I have learned of so many people and friends who have suffered for so long in their marriages, and honestly, they may have even gone to their clergy. Still, they are not happy.

Satan knows his time is short and so his biggest attack, as we know, is the family. But when you look at the number of husbands and wives that struggle in their marriages because they don't know how to fix it, it's incredible! And they think they're the only ones in this dark place.

And they've got temple covenants to think about. What are they going to do?

In my early 20s, when I made the choice to come back to Heavenly Father, I had a powerful experience, one that I had heard of others having but now it became a reality for me. I was being overcome by Satan, laying in my bed in my studio apartment with the darkness closing in. The feeling was so heavy that I couldn't breathe.

I heard him say, "I will have you."

And in that exact moment, I called upon God. It was a real deal, a very real, frightening deal. In that terrible moment I was given strength to overcome.

Here is the absolute, most marvelous news. We have a Savior who performed an atonement and restored the gospel of Jesus Christ that opened up blessings, giving us the power to overcome anything. This includes looking at our personalities, our differences, to connect us even closer to one another; Satan is using our personalities, our differences, to separate us, fool and trick us.

Yes, Satan is using our personalities, our differences, to separate us. But what if we accepted our differences? Embraced our personalities? Not the weaknesses thereof but the strengths? What if Heavenly Father embraces our strengths and lifts us through them and Satan uses our weaknesses to suppress our strengths?

It may take a long time, and part of it will be painful. But how can our Father not be there 24/7 to help us? How can anyone think that there is anything between us and God but heaven 24/7?

Satan will attack. His time is short. But our time is eternal. Return to the path. On the path your differences can become great strengths! Stay on the path, hold tight to His hand. It may seem to take a long time, and parts may be painful because we decide to be in the cave or stay too long in the comfortable house, but we can always return to the path.

Our Father is always there 24/7 to help us on the path. There is nothing between us and Heavenly Father but 24/7 care.

Kathryn

I like my comfortable home. Although the darkness of the cave rarely surrounds me for long, I like being in comfort.

And that's why I enjoy my home.

But the Lord wants something greater for me than a new rug or a recently framed picture. He wants me to have a place to hear Him, yes, but he also wants me to venture out.

As a child and teenager I was a loner. For me, being in my childhood home was a comfort, a place to steal away and to be myself. I knew my family loved me. I knew this. But the people out there? Well, that was another story.

When Doug came into my life, let's just say I was surprised. Why would a tall and handsome man be interested in a skinny, ugly young woman?

I couldn't believe it. I also couldn't believe he wanted to date me. But I think, by then, I was aching to get out of that often visited dark cave, and that beautiful safe house that my mother had created, and do something with my life! And somehow, deep down inside, I knew this young man would help me.

And he did.

I learned that I had talents. I learned that I could write. And this man helped me along the way and still does when I find myself returning to the dark cave for a little pity party. I go there because I remember how it all was before my mother divorced her first husband, my father, and married the second. I remember the aching nights when she and my father fought behind closed doors. I remembered the days when they wouldn't speak to one another. I remember being in a home where the silence was deadly and most of my happiest moments were spent behind a good book.

The divorce of my parents was a good thing, I can see that now, but then, I grew lost and afraid of my own abilities to function in the world. I learned to hide.

No one really wants to live in the dark cave. But there is something you need to know about it. If you feel you're alone, you must know that you are not. There are others, like you and unlike you, who are searching for the hand that's reaching out.

Do you see Him?

I didn't for a very, very long time.

When my mother re-married, things were much better for me. The house no longer felt silent. People spoke to one another, hugged one another, but still, there was something deep inside me that I couldn't let go of.

As I search now in my adulthood, I often wonder what really held me back, what kept me in the house of introspection and hiding for so long.

Was it fear of the unknown? Was it lack of trust in myself or others that kept me there? Was it my lack of faith that I would still sometimes return to that dark place, the cave?

Probably. Most definitely.

And yet, there's a man in white with an outstretched hand. He is waiting for me to see Him, to find Him. He won't push His way into my life, but He is there waiting for me to ask.

We all have a path to travel, and your path will never be the same as mine. You may travel the path of neglect or abuse, or you may travel the path of loneliness. But whatever your path, whatever is strewn along the way - weeds or flowers, or a little bit of both - know that the Lord is there waiting for you to take His hand once again, and journey on the path.

- What have you discovered about your own house? Your own path? The cave of darkness in which you may sit?
- Are you ready to be carried up the mountain?

The

Basement

The Basement

What are your emotional attachments?

Imagine that you're in a basement, but no ordinary basement.

This basement with its four cement walls and solid floors houses only one object.

A bathtub.

You see the bathtub from a distance, an old thing, with claws for feet, and rusted turn on valves, once gold, now corroded with green and black slime.

The tub's not filled with water. The smells tell you that. The stuff inside is brown and moldy; refuge of some sort. It wafts to your nostrils and causes you to cough.

You look down. Sure enough, the tub is filled with refuse; your refuse, from your own body. The thought sickens you even as you look down at it, wondering and wondering again why *that* instead of the water that might be inside.

Well, why not *that*?

I have often thought of sin as the refuge I carry. Like the stone, mentioned in a previous *glimpse*, sin is carried when it is better off cleansed. Sin is kept within the vehicle, the very vehicle that is meant to wash us clean.

So, why do we keep it there?

Why do we let sin sit and smolder below our very noses?

I know why I do it.

Because I feel as if I have every right to. Because the other person has hurt me. Because it's their fault. Because I'm too afraid to go to God and ask forgiveness. Because the sin is too big. Because...

I'm sure you have your reasons.

Just as I have mine.

This I know. The longer I decide not to use the power of the atonement, the harder it becomes to clean out the tub; the more difficult it becomes to turn on the knobs.

Or so it seems.

Unless...

Of course there is one, and only one who knows how to clean out my tub, to turn on the unyielding knobs, to release me from the filthy burden.

Like a tub without water, we may be searching for healing, but forgetting from whence the healing must come.

We have pains and wounds but refuse to be healed.

And yet, there is the tub and the One who has the power to clean the tub if we request it of Him.

Like the stone, the basement of our lives houses a tub of cleansing. When we are ready, the Lord is there for cleansing and healing. Sometimes the healing comes early, at other times, it comes after years of suffering.

Why?

How else would we learn who we are and who God is? How else could we ultimately learn what it takes to live life?

Because only God can change our heart, and only *we* can allow the process to take place, He waits until we are ready to let go of the emotional attachment.

Kathryn

I have a negative emotional attachment associated with people who can't seem to control themselves. The more severe or consistent the problem, the greater my emotional attachment - I just have to hang on to it.

This problem of control manifested itself profoundly when, a few years ago, a relative attacked my husband. (I have told a portion of this story under the chapter entitled, "A Stone"). The wounds in his head were severe. The outer scars still remain, but quite amazingly, my husband was able to forgive the perpetrator early on.

I wanted the man to go to jail for a very, very long time.

I thought about the terrible incident for days, and my heart was sick inside. *How could I let this feeling go?*

It was then a voice said, *"I can take it."*

I knew who the voice belonged to. I'd heard Him through the years, speaking to me when I was finally quiet in body and spirit to hear Him. But I wasn't sure if I wanted to give it - to give in. The perpetrator deserved a heavy sentence. He deserved to be in jail.

We went to court, my heart still full of the emotional attachment associated with the perpetrator's lack of self-control. I didn't know if I could do it.

And then I saw him.

He was standing near the window, right by the doors to the courtroom. *"I can't do this anymore,"* I whispered in my heart. The pain was too heavy. I'd only been weighed down for a few weeks since the incident, but my heart felt as heavy as if I'd been carrying the stone for years.

That's when it came. A sort of wave sensation, that began at my feet and rushed up my body to my head and out. I looked at the perpetrator again, and suddenly, almost without warning, I saw him differently. It was almost as if he was a different person standing there, though on reflection, I realized that he was the same - I was different. On reaching him, we embraced. He didn't say he was sorry. He didn't say anything, but the forgiveness was complete.

Because of my husband's compassion the man was given a lighter sentence of community service. He was able to leave the courtroom with his family. He was able to begin his life again.

No, I have never received an apology. He has never sought me or my husband out to ask us to forgive him, but something about that moment, that eternal 24/7 moment, has changed me forever.

Celeste

Sin, ahhhh, Sin. That thing that comes in so many sizes, small, medium, large; so many colors, white, gray, yellow, scarlet; so many forms, big and fat, thinly lined, over indulged, well hidden, covered and protected by other actions, masked in thought, kept behind a closed door or even our closed heart. Yes…that thing. We all know it in some form or fashion. AND, God knows it—24/7. Yes, you're right, it's gonna happen, more than once. Our Creator knows that also.

So, why is it that we insist on keeping it? Sin. Well, to name a few "reasons" "rationales" and "excuses" that I've attempted in my life to keep and cover my own sins, let's take a look at: embarrassment, fear, pride, shame, hurt feelings, anger, poor self-esteem, judgment, lack of faith, self-pity, feelings of entitlement, blame, and on, and on, and on, blah blah blah blah blah...

I love Kathryn's visual metaphor of the bathtub in the basement.

Many years ago, when a young woman, I discovered that I had a tub full of refuse (I wrote about some of this time back in our chapter on Stones). My tub was a full, putrid mess of sin. When my heart's desire became greater and stronger than the mess in my tub, I realized I needed to seriously clean it! But, I could only do so much to clean it. I could remove the contents that were creating the refuse but I could not remove the stains, the pitting, the holes, the rust, the buildup and an odor that had touched other's lives, at least not alone anyway. I had to take my tub to a master cleaner.

Shame, fear, embarrassment…oh yes, I had these in abundance. I needed to take this filthy tub to the master cleaner's shop where his front line associate could assess the damage. It was the only way.

It was soooo heavy carrying that tub to the shop. My legs were shaky, my heart pounding, my head screaming *"What are you doing! Do you know what could happen in that shop?"*

But, I did it! It was harder carrying the tub full of stuff around than carrying it in to have it assessed. I was so embarrassed and fearful to uncover my tub. It was interesting to me, though. Even with the embarrassment and fear, there was an element of trust. I realized I wanted to trust the master cleaner and his associate. That inkling of trust was coming from my heart's desire which was stronger than my shaking body and screaming head.

I revealed most of this refuse that had been in my tub and the damage the refuse had caused not only to me but to others; the associate listened intently as if every thought and word I spoke was being looked at, weighed, and measured, for they were. That's how the associates work. They listen deeply for our hearts to reveal themselves.

We sat for a time, quiet, while the associate completed his assessment. He then asked if I understood how deep the damage was that I had created. He asked what I had done and would do to repair that damage. He asked what I had done with the contents of the tub. I responded to each query with humble confidence. Humbled because of all the damage I had created, yet confident because of the strength of the desire in my heart. I had followed my heart's desire and I would not go back to carrying that tub! The associate knew it. The master cleaner knew it.

And then, as if the master cleaner had suddenly joined us in the shop, his associate informed me that the master cleaner had granted me a new tub, clean and ready to be refurbished with new porcelain, a protective coating, and polishing. And, the associate had been given the instructions on how each application was to be done. We would work together, he and I, to create a beautiful new tub with golden feet.

Golden feet that I stand on to this day!

I have learned much since that horrible bathtub. And, over the years, I have found new refuse trying to grow and multiply in my tub. But I still stand on golden feet and I have learned and continue to learn how to clean my tub. I have grown to love the master cleaner's associates. They are a wonderful resource when I need them.

The best part is, I have learned to hear and recognize the master cleaner's voice and his instructions. I have learned to seek for it, listen for it, and do my best to heed its whisperings. I am still learning this, I am still a novice, but the master is patient.

- Do you have a bathtub in your basement?
- Do you want to see and smell what's in your tub?
- What condition is it in?
- Might it need to be cleaned? Do you know how to clean your tub? Does it possibly need to go to the shop?
- Are you ready to take it in?
- Would you trust the associate? And if not, why?

- What "reasons" rationales" and "excuses" might you be using to hide your bathtub?
- Does your heart desire the master cleaner's touch? How strong is that desire?
- Do you know that He already knows the condition of your bathtub?
- Do you remember him? He asked us to do that you know. Do you seek to hear Him and follow his instructions?
- Do you know that the master cleaner loves and cheers for the novice? And, he will be patient?

The

Garden

The Garden

What do you grow?

Imagine you've planted a garden. And it's a successful garden that produces tomatoes, cucumbers, radishes, watermelons, cantaloupes, everything you love.

Now think for a minute about your harvest.

Imagine that you have so much harvest that you can fit it all, every bit of it, into the trunk of your car. Even after you have shared with your family and have given to others, you are left with this abundance. It never depletes.

But you don't share it. You leave these fruits and vegetables to their own desires. And what are these desires?

Fruit flies.

Rot.

Mold.

You have forgotten they are there. Maybe you knew they were there but you didn't want to be bothered with them so you shut the lid.

You shut the lid.

There are times in my own family, even in my extended family, where I've shut the lid to listening, time, experiences, helpfulness, gratitude. And you know, it's hurt me.

But, I reason to myself, I was hurt first. And so, to protect myself from further pain I have shut the lid and figuratively allowed my family to rot in there without me.

Dreams are like that. They show you what you don't want to see in the light of day. They express to you your darkest thoughts, your deepest pains.

But they also show you something else. What you can do about it.

When a fruit or vegetable is picked, before the worms get to it, what do you do with it? You wash and eat it. You may even deliver it to an unsuspecting neighbor; especially if the vegetable is the coveted zucchini.

Would you purposely let your fruits and vegetables rot in the trunk of your car or on the kitchen counter?

It's amazing what can rot in plain sight isn't it?

By the end of September, vegetables are shooting forth faster than you can eat them. So you bottle and freeze and give them as gifts, though some of them manage to spoil before your very eyes.

Kathryn

I am often like the rotten fruit, wondering why *I* smell.

Will I forgive an older relative - not my husband - who has never grown up, whom I feel as if I have to take care of every time I'm with him? Am I up for another embarrassing episode with a waitress, because he thinks he is being *cute*? Am I willing to take my life into my hands when he drives me in his car, when he thinks that he's the only other person on the road, and that somehow, weaving in and out of traffic and getting angry at everyone else on the street, somehow lets him off the dangerous - hook? Will I remain smiling when this same relative flirts with my sisters or my daughters?

I can tell you what I did do.

After weeks and years of trying and failing to make our relationship work, I said, *enough is enough.* I didn't forgive him, I separated myself from him. I kept myself away from the embarrassment of him. From the fear of him.

I have done the same with others in my life, whom I believe have crossed the line. I said *enough is enough* to a girlfriend with depression and physical issues - much of which she couldn't control.

I have carried this pain for a long time, along with the pain of other friends who decided, quite frankly, that I wasn't worth their time - they were better off without me. I decided the same thing with another loved one who preferred speaking about me behind my back rather than facing me with questions of the heart.

For years, and for more days than I'd like to count, I have felt the burden of the spoiling fruit and vegetables. I have literally shut the lid and allowed the fruit to spoil.

Forgiving someone of their sin or weakness may possibly never be easy for me, whether what they are struggling with is sin or weakness, because it often feels the same to me. I am filled with anger and resentment. I want them to change. Get better. Be better.

But the Lord asks me to do something else. He asks me to change myself.

How do I do that? How do I change myself when I'm not feeling 24/7?

Previously in this book, I referred to stone carrying. I spoke of meeting God at a lake and handing him the stone you are carrying. As you may remember, you couldn't just throw the stone into the water and call it good. Though the stone would be at the bottom of the lake, it would still be there. You couldn't hit the person with it, because, especially then, the stone would still be there for both of you. But some stones are harder to let go of.

Recall what God said: *"I am here, when you're ready."*

We aren't always ready to let go of some of the stones we carry. These stones may be terrific boulders filled with years of built up pain. Though I had let go of some of the stones mentioned above, the idea of letting go of one of them, isn't yet in my heart - yet. Changing myself, in this area at least, is going to be a slower process, a pulling away of many layers, until the heart of the matter is discovered. What I know is God is ready and willing to take my stone when I am ready to let it go, and love me just the same until I do it.

So what do you do when you're not feeling heaven 24/7, when you're not willing to give up the huge boulder in your own life?

I'd like to think prayer is a huge answer. We are commanded to love our enemies, and the greatest form of love is forgiveness. Still, there may be times in your own life when the boulder is so huge (maybe even the weeds in your garden are so thick), the layers so deep, the questions so confusing, you may opt out on the final and complete answer - at least for now.

But if you are praying always, seeking for ways to finally hand the boulder to him, asking him to remove the layers of pain, guilt and shame that wrap around you like a tourniquet, there will come a day, when through your faithfulness, your drawing closer to Christ, your seeking for change, and his ultimate and tender mercy, that the change will come. And you will feel it like a burning bush.

This I know for sure.

Celeste

I love to garden. I don't do it as much as I used to. But, when I do, oh how I revel in it. The soil preparation, rich, dark, ready to receive and nurture the seeds and infant plants. Planning each row so that every seed and plant will have room and be able to grow to its fullest. Watering, weeding, pruning as each seedling gains strength from the mother soil and matures. And then, the flower, the fruit, the glory of it all.

I am an excellent gardener. I have produced many a splendid garden with an abundant bounty in the fall. I have nurtured my gardens. Talked with them. Sung to them. Cared for them. Praised them for their gifts. Knelt in deep gratitude for the earth, seed, and fruit, the miracle thereof.

At times there has been disease that has struck my garden. I have had to remove the diseased plant(s) to protect the healthy. Sad. Many I have worked to save but they did not respond to my efforts.

Weeds, they grow in a garden.

Weeds, they grow in relationships.

It has taken me quite some time to recognize the weeds that can grow in my relationships. Blame, anger, distrust, envy, laziness, frustration, inflexible expectation, perfectionism, to identify a few of the culprits. Like all weeds they start as a tiny seedling. Yet, if not watched for and guarded against, they grow ever so strong and prolific! Even out of control.

So what do weeds and relationships have to do with living heaven 24/7?

EVERYTHING!

I finally started to get it, understand it, and recognize my role as the gardener in every relationship I am blessed to have. I am responsible for the garden. I am responsible for its care. I am responsible for its growth. I am responsible for the fruit it will bear. I am responsible for removing the weeds.

About a year ago now I was blessed with a beautiful tender mercy, a calling to repentance of sorts. I was having an extreme struggle with an intimate, close relationship. The magnitude of a relationship that, if lost, could rip a hole in many, many lives.

One day as I was working, things around me became still and it was as if I was experiencing a dream – during the middle of the day – a daydream per se. There was myself and two others in the dream. In the imagery of the setting, it felt as though I was in the presence of two supreme beings. Warm, loving, complete. Many things were discussed amongst the three of us. I vividly recall being chastened for how I was viewing the relationship I had been struggling with. How the only view I was focused on was my own. How unfair that was, how selfishly inwardly focused that was. Did I not realize that I had been given this relationship to nurture? To water, prune, protect from weeds, feed, strengthen, talk and sing to, love? Did I not realize that this relationship that had been planted in nutrient rich soil with everything required, if it was tended properly, had the potential to produce the most glorious of all fruits?

Oh foolish one! The outcome of this garden, this relationship was up to me!

An intense sense of love and gratitude filled every fiber of my being. A feeling of confidence, not coming from me but confidence being poured into me, showed me that I would be able to weed my garden and remove from me the weeds that had grown. As I turned outward and my view was corrected, I would see how to nurture, strengthen, and grow my garden, my relationship. I was filled with hope and joy.

As I have continued to apply what I was instructed in that daydream, I have reaped the blessings as told. My relationship has grown strong, healthy, powerful.

But first, I had to be the excellent gardener. And, I continue to be because there will always be weeds!

I AM THE GARDENER!

I recently received some wonderful reminders of this lesson through a mentor of mine. To paraphrase: in order for things to change, I must change, in order for anything to get better, I must get better. How many people does it take to have a relationship? One.

This is another evidence of living connected to heaven 24/7. Continued education and support there from. I am never alone when I am seeking and listening. Heaven is always there.

- What about you? Have you learned to be an excellent gardener?
- Do you have weeds? Careful now. Be sure you are looking for your own weeds in order to be able to properly nurture your gardens.
- What of your family?
- Who amongst the many, needs your fruit?
- Who's fruit, amongst the many, do you need to accept?

The

Window

The Window

What do you really want?

Imagine you're standing inside a large home that rests on a mountain hilltop. You know this because outside the window you can see the sky and trees and a million flowers instead of cars and high rise buildings.

You are standing in the living room, at its center. At your feet is a map of the world; to the right, rooms in need of construction. A door is missing, or maybe a wall or the wall-to-wall carpeting. In front of you is a large window, large enough to see out to the furthest outskirts. There is no one out here - but you.

Still, your arms are outstretched as if waiting for someone to enter, to give you hope, a hug.

It is mid-day. The warmth coming through the window warms your face, your arms, your bare feet. The map at your feet blazes in light, and you wonder why it is there, why you are here in this exact spot, what the workers have been doing inside the house and when the house will be completed.

All is silent as you stand there. There are no workers today. There is no reason to clean. There is no one in the house but you.

There is nothing for you to do but stand there and reflect on your life in the world.

You feel His presence, though you do not see Him. You know you are loved, though, in that moment He does not tell you so in words. You wonder again about the rooms in need of repair.

You know, as you stand there facing the window of light, that this is the focus He wants for you. Even in construction, with plenty of fix-ups to come, He will help you remember the direction He would like you to face on this earth. And the light through the window will help you remember He is there.

I am incomplete and He is my construction manager.

Kathryn

In my own life it's easy to forget the truth of what's real in favor of the day to day tasks of living. After all, it's the tangible things I *see* that often take precedence over the things I *feel*.

Is it that way with you?

Read my scriptures? I have dishes to do. Work on my Sunday lesson? I have errands to run. Spend time with the Lord?

There is just too much to do.

Isn't it interesting that the Lord doesn't shout? I only remember one time in the scriptures when he even got mad. When he cleansed the temple at Jerusalem. Remember how he had that great whip and how he knocked down the money changer's tables, and drove out all of the animals?

Who wouldn't do the same if someone was selling their wares instead of doing what they should have been doing in the first place - worshipping God? The house wasn't just any house, it was the temple, and the people knew it, though they had obviously forgotten the truth of the matter in favor of something else.

Is your home your temple?
What takes precedence within it?

As a writer, it is often difficult for me to set aside my writing in favor of the better thing, and I find that I have to remind myself (like now) that it is God who has given me the gift. It's far too easy for me to think about how to market my next book, or write that next scene, or gather up my things for the next book signing.

Through all my daily tasks, whatever they are, it's also up to me to stand at the window of light and receive of Him.

Like the house in the above scenario, I am often in need of repair. The world, with all of its flashing lights and glimmering entertainment has replaced my center - if only briefly. But if I let go of my agenda and the world's expectations and humble myself before Him, I see that He is bidding me to the window.

Celeste

Noise, hustle and bustle, hurry, time is ticking. My list, where is my list? What's next?....and on, and on, and on. Oh life, what are you truly for?

I had an experience, an "awake dream" I'll call it since I wasn't day dreaming nor was I asleep. It was just there, many years ago in which I found myself, as a little girl, maybe 3 or 4 years old, playing and dancing in a pillar of light. The surroundings were darkened.

Yet, there was a light beam that came from somewhere that seemed to have no beginning to somewhere that had no end. There I was, in the center of that glorious column of light, reveling in it, laughing and giggling and reaching up, arms stretched high above my head. Swaying and flowing with the light as if it were a pillar of pure energy filling every fiber of my existence and flowing through me. The light was shimmering, sparkling, white, gold, and silver, warm and ever so completing. That was it! I was complete. My joy was so full being in the light. Oh it was so exquisite.

I am learning more and more, every day, that is what life is for. To dance in the light and be filled. All of the daily routine, all of the "have to's", "must do's", "do now's", scream loudly and demand attention. I cannot face them without the light. They will crush me, overtake me, and eventually I will lose me.

What do I want? The light. To be filled with the light. To be always connected to the light.

And so I seek the light. That is my priority above all else. I have chosen to make it so.

How?

Well, life does have its demands and they do get to be met. But, I go to the window first thing in my days and last thing in my nights. I have learned that *I* have the power to go to the window and dance in the light.

I begin my days very early. The light is bright early in the morning, well before the sun comes up and the world awakens. I pray. I ask if there are specific instructions for me that day. I look at my dreams and goals and ponder them. And, I dance. Not just any dance but a light gathering dance. This is sacred time. It is a very small sacrifice, being up long before the sun raises its head, to bask in the light and be clothed in its armor.

Face the day, the noise, hustle and bustle? Oh yes. I have my armor on…

Then comes the closing of my day, after the noise, hustle and bustle has possibly dented, cracked, and marred my armor. The light awaits. I pray, giving thanks and gratitude for the armor that has seen me through my day, taken the arrows for me. I read of others experiences with the light and how they, throughout history, were led and guided by the light. And then I remember again my dreams and goals and what my life is truly about and I ponder. Dance, yes. This dance though is a dance of healing, feeling the rhythm of the light and allowing it to smooth and repair my armor. Flowing, soothing, nurturing. The light is soft, candle light softness, peaceful, calm. A hug and kiss good night from Heaven. The light is always there. Learn to go to the window. *You* have the power to do so.

- What gets in your way of doing the most important things first?

93

- What replaces your desires to get to know the Lord better?
- What excuses do you use to put off what you know will help you in drawing closer to the Lord - today?
- What do you do or can you do each day to help you come to the light?
- When are you "still" and able to hear the call to the window?
- When do you or can you create a moment to be filled and healed by the light?
- When do you or can you DANCE in the light that comes through your window?
- Remember, YOU have the power to go to the window and dance!

Diamonds

Diamonds

How do you see yourself?

Imagine for a moment that you've just lost the diamond from your wedding ring. You are distraught. You look through closets, drawers, underneath sofas, even inside the sink (you hope it's not there because if it is it's probably down the drain).

You look everywhere you think it will be; even some places where you're sure it's not, only to come away empty handed.

You look down at your ring. The hole where the diamond should be is about as glaring as the struggles that have attached themselves to your life. You don't know what to do.

And then it comes.

Pray.

Your first thought is that you feel like a child. But you do it.

Moments later you feel the need to look once more in the couch cushions.

There, you find it.

You are overjoyed.

You promise yourself that you're going to take the ring in and have the prongs fixed. For now, you'll just put the diamond back inside the ring until you can get to it.

A few weeks later, you look down at your hand.

Lost, again!

You go in search of the diamond, only this time you remember to pray sooner, and listening to the direction of God you find the diamond within the weaves of the living room carpet, in the very spot you thought you'd just checked.

Now you know how important it is to get the ring fixed.

Instead of wearing it, however, you place the ring and the diamond in a small Ziploc bag, and into your jewelry box. You think to yourself, *now the diamond won't get lost.*

And it doesn't. But it does sit in your jewelry box for another 10 years. Sight unseen. Problem covered. Out of sight, out of mind, right?

Struggles, at least in my life, are kind of like that. Time may not heal all wounds after all. The minutes, hours, days and years may simply be hiding them away. And if I am not careful, watchful, prayerful, I may find that the wounds are still *there*, glaring at me from inside the jewelry box.

Prayer is a wonderful ointment, but to be completely healed, the diamond put back in place on the ring finger - whole - one must consider what it means to look inside yourself, take a step out of your comfort zone and make a personal shift, a positive shift to God.

Kathryn

I was a pretty shy girl; most of my friends were shy along with me, and I only had a few. If someone asked me a question, I cowered. If I was asked to speak in class, I whispered. If someone called me "skinny" I cried. I hid.

Once, only once mind you, I told someone they were fat. But that was after they'd told me I was skinny. They got mad. They thought being skinny was a far cry different from being fat, and proceeded to lecture me on what was worse.

Once I was at a bus stop and a boy was looking over my shoulder to see what books I was carrying. Only someone had to make a crude comment, and then another was made to my shame: "Well, she doesn't have anything to look at anyway."

Sometimes we carry ourselves as if we're still that teen girl trying to find herself. We walk around the planet hoping someone will notice us, someone will like us, someone will encourage us instead of tear us down. We hope, no pray, that we no longer look skinny or flat- chested to others who are far more endowed than we are. We hope we have changed, that we've somehow, moved on.

And then it comes. The remark that reminds us of yesterday.

Do we see ourselves as a diamond? Imperfect, yes, but a diamond, even a "diamond in the rough"? Why is it that we can't accept ourselves for who we are and the gifts and talents we've been given? When did looks become so all-fire important?

I'm no longer young, but there are some that would still call me, thin, maybe even flat-chested. Still, where once was smooth skin there are wrinkles. My hair is graying and my hands are starting to get those wicked brown spots - I call them 'wicked' because they weren't invited. Sometimes, when I look in the mirror, I see this older woman. I wonder, "where am I?" and I turn away from myself wishing I was young again.

Where are you?

What is the most important thing about you? Is it your weight? Your body type? Your skin? Your hair? Your clothes?

I hope not.

That diamond that each of us most assuredly is, is waiting. Yes, we may yet be a *diamond in the rough* waiting for our heavenly ascent, but we are God's daughters. His diamonds.

His.

Celeste

Oh, how I love Kathryn! She is so elegant and eloquent in her writing and in who she is. So descriptive. Me, well I'm me. And I'm good with that. And I mean that in a very good, confident way. We, Kathryn and I, are very different...in writing styles and in appearance. Yet, this I know, we are both diamonds!

I have struggled the greater part of my sixty year life with weight, the heavier side thereof. It is what is with my body. I've spanned the distance between a svelte and sexy 150 lbs, wearing a size 8, to surpassing 300 lbs, still sexy (so my wonderful and wise husband said), but not wearing a size 8. Talk about having reason to have a few self-image challenges!

I have been blessed though throughout my life. My true self-image has been attached to deeper core beliefs than my weight. Now, please don't get me wrong. I have continually sought for answers to this whole weight thing. As I've gotten older it's become more of a health factor. At sixty I'm not going to find that twenty year old body, ho hum. But good news…I can and am finding a healthy sixty year old body! Yeah!

I do want to share a little message I received not long ago. It's kind of important. But before I share that, let me go back to Kathryn's beautiful analogy of the diamond ring and prayer. You see, I lost the diamond from my wedding ring once back in about 1996.

I was working for a satellite company on the southern coast of Oregon. I was in the office one day doing what I was there for, working. While working I saw it, the hole! My diamond was gone! Panic set in. My wedding set is a one of a kind German setting in which a specific type of diamond was used. Replacing it would not be the easiest thing.

Now, because my main diamond is not really large, it was not something that was going to "stand out" wherever it was lost.

Did I pray, oh yes. Did I find, miraculously, yes. And then, just as in Kathryn's allegory, I put it away, for 15 plus years.

Through the years I'd take my ring out of its protective envelope and think about what it represented, love. I would tell myself, "I really need to get this repaired," then I'd put it away and close the drawer.

Well, going on two years ago now, I took my beautiful ring out, looked at it, felt the emotion of deep love that it represented, and promptly took it to the jeweler to have it repaired! I was tired of feeling incomplete. I was tired of the appearance that I was only a single wedding band without diamonds.

No, no, no, do not go there. There is nothing wrong or inadequate about a single wedding band. That is not what I'm getting at.

My point is that I felt incomplete, my appearance was not complete.

So, coming forward to today with my experience with weight and appearances. Just as it took *me* to finally repair my ring and reunite it with my wedding band, I have always desired to be one with my weight. I've lost it and found it more than once. So I decided to pray, differently this time though.

Yes, I talked with Heavenly Father. It was interesting. I had been learning about a technique, a mentoring tool, used to assist people in looking inside for answers to their own questions. It has been shown to be quite effective. So the thought came, *use this tool*.

I decided on my way to work a few weeks ago to have a conversation with myself, utilizing the tool I had learned about. I started by envisioning myself in the car seat next to me. (I have not lost it…it's a tool) Then I asked myself if it was okay for us to have a discussion. I imagined that myself answered in the affirmative. And so I began the conversation.

Me: "You know I've been working on our weight for years. Trying to find the keys to a permanent, healthy weight. I've learned so much that I am grateful for. Yet, there is still this missing link to making it permanent. Can you help me out with this? Why is being at a healthy weight, notice I didn't say perfect weight, so elusive?"

Myself responding to me: "Well, think about it. If you want to be lighter you need to live lighter."

Me: "What?"

Myself: "You need to be happy. You need to get rid of things in your life that weigh you down. What makes you think that carrying around heavy stuff, emotions, would not manifest in your physical life?"

Me: Light bulb on…"it's that easy?"

Myself: "Yes. Remove things from your life that are not necessary and weighing you down. Then, find happy things. Find happy music. Music moves you. It will support you. You must choose to be happy…with yourself, Celeste."

Now, this simple exercise has changed me, internally. I went on in the conversation to make a commitment, a contract you might say, with myself, to eat what is good for my body and myself agreed to assist in removing the weight. That simple gesture of making that contract with myself has been of great support when I could have been tempted to eat not so well.

So, why do I tell you this story when we're talking about diamonds, appearances, and heaven 24/7?

Because how we think and see ourselves matters and affects our lives! The scriptures tell us, and I paraphrase: *As a man thinketh, so is he.*

Your worth is not defined by your appearance!

Are you willing to put yourself in a chair, face yourself, and ask questions?

No, you're not crazy if you do. You may find some interesting answers.

By the way, I've lost 8 lbs since that conversation. Haven't changed anything except I have an awesome "happy music" play list...

- Are you happy with *you*? Have a conversation with yourself. Write everything down as you experience it.

Ownership

Ownership

Do you find your answers from deep within?

Imagine that you're in a large room. It is lit up with a bright light on the ceiling, it's tendrils casting warmth onto your arms and face. You should be joyous, but you are not. The walls are a dull-gray color, and as you stand there, in the middle of the room searching for an answer to why you are there, the walls seem to say, "Who do you think you are anyway?"

You do not know. You stand there for some time, and the idea of the room depresses you. There is no place to sit. No carpet. No window. And the walls are depressing. But there is that bright light above you.

One day you notice a little tear in the gray wall, and realize that the wall is not painted gray, it is papered. You tear a piece of the gray from the corner where it is coming loose from the wall, and continue to tear, until all four walls are no longer gray, but yellow.

Imagine! Under all that gray paper there was a yellow flowered pattern! Who knows how long it had been there, waiting for you to find. You stand in the

111

self-same room, and everything has changed, though only a layer of paper has been removed.

Oh, but what a layer!

Celeste

What will others think of me?

Oh, the insidiousness of that question!

It's easy to say, *"Well, it doesn't matter what others think of me"* in theory. Few of us actually ignore that voice that helps us filter our thoughts and words. And that's a good thing. We do get to be respectful of others and respected by others. But that question of *"what will others think of me"* can be quite the oppressive master if I let it go - unchecked.

Several years ago I found myself searching, pondering, questioning: Just who am I? What on earth am I supposed to be doing? Do I really matter in the grand scheme of things? How can I possibly influence anything or anyone? I pondered and asked and pondered and asked.

Then I listened:

"Celeste, you are a powerful, passionate, creative woman."

Powerful…Passionate…Creative. Each rang true to the depths of my soul.

It continued. *"You have a purpose in being a powerful, passionate, creative woman to create excellence, magnificence, joy and light in not only your own life but in the lives of others."*

And so, my personal creation statement began. I will not quote my statement in its entirety as it is rather personal, sacred in a sense, to me. I do desire to share an experience with you though that I hope will help you to find in you your creation statement, if you have not already done so, and encourage you to live it...in spite of what others may think, or you may think they think.

In my traditional and my entrepreneurial business lives I found myself struggling; struggling with self-esteem for a period of time. As I look back, it was not just in my business life that this struggle was happening, it was in my life in general. I was wrestling with this word "powerful". I knew the attribute to be true of me. It was alive inside of me, deep in my core. I could not deny its existence. On some level, though, I seemed to be afraid of it.

One evening I brought this quandary to my husband's attention in conversation. He so often can see things clearly when I do not.

I am learning to appreciate him more and more for his insights.

So, I told him of my fear of this quality of being "powerful". How I realized that I was afraid of stepping into and exhibiting that powerful part of me...because of what others might think of me. I didn't want others to feel I might be putting myself above them, or looking down at them, or that I was trying to elevate myself. I didn't want anyone to feel small or inadequate in my presence.

I have experienced this on too many occasions. Case in point: I am a singer. Heavenly Father has given me the gift to express my heart through a beautiful voice. At times others have expressed their feeling of being inadequate as singers when performing either in a choir I was directing or performing with me on a program, because of the quality of my voice. They felt they were not good enough, their talent not as good as mine. Oh, if they only knew how devastating that type of comment is to me! Yes, God has given me the gift of voice and expression with that gift. But I have been given that gift to lift and elevate others, never to downgrade or make small. For others to compare their talent to anyone else's, including mine, is painful for me. We are all given talents in varying forms and degrees. All are just as vital as any other. All are to be celebrated. And so, at times, "what others thought of me" became an oppressive challenge, causing me to shrink from sharing and giving that gift.

I found this fear manifesting in my business life as well. That shrinking away from the powerful business woman that I am. I have knowledge and information that can assist others in their lives. *Why on earth would I not share that! Why would I choose to not help someone when I could see that what I have to offer could bring aid to their lives?* Possibly because of "what others might think of me?"

My husband, in his wisdom, recognized a valuable insight that I had not. He saw the flaw in my thinking. I was viewing the attribute of being "powerful" as exactly what I did not want it to be, oppressive, putting down. You know, the overlord type. Oh my goodness!!! No wonder others would make those comments to me. They were only mirroring back to me what I was fearful of in myself!

My husband then helped me to learn a valuable lesson: reframing and ownership. What if the attribute of being "powerful" is not oppressive? What if it is "influence" instead? Ahhhhhh, that struck a chord of truth. Deep truth. I can be, and am, powerful in influencing others to be excellent, magnificent, joyful and filled with light. That is what I strive to bring to others. That is a part of my purpose.

How can I shrink from that gift? Be smaller than divinely designed for? My gift is not something to fear. It is a gift to serve with. Taking ownership and stewardship of that attribute is where the power lies. The power to lift, encourage, inspire.

The magnificent opening lines of the familiar Marianne Williamson poem reads: *"Our deepest fear is not that we are inadequate. Our deepest fear is that we are powerful beyond measure."*

Truer words have rarely been penned. Living in the light of heaven 24/7 can bring to us the truth of who we are. Yes, there may be mirrors all around us to assist us in seeing clearly. Helping us to reframe, to view ourselves properly.

Ownership.

Have you struggled with the fear of being who you are designed to be? Do you fear what others may think when you know of your gifts and talents?

Ponder.

Ask.

Reframe.

Take ownership and BE.

Kathryn

Years ago I came up with my own mission statement and then promptly went about my life. In time I forgot the words I'd promised to remember and live. Even as I read Celeste's journey with her own mission statement, I thought, *"Well, I don't remember mine."*

I felt bad that I hadn't remembered, and yet, I also knew that years had gone by and that I'd shelved the words away, thinking that they didn't need to be out in the open for me to remember them.

How wrong I was.

In process of time, the words I had once held close to my heart evaporated, like water on warm pavement. I no longer thought of them, but once in awhile a comment would spark the memory and I would wonder again about the words. *What had I told myself so long ago? What was it that had prompted me to write the words, and what were they?*

I continued to wonder until this morning. And then, like the rising of the sun, the words came: "Kathy, you are a beautiful, caring and trusting woman."

So that was it.

After so many years away from my mission I realized it had been there all along. Though not consciously remembered, there yet remained those heart-felt thoughts within my soul, just waiting for the right moment to be released.

This was that moment.

I was still that beautiful, caring and trusting woman that I had been so many years ago. I could still see it.

- Is this your moment? Can you see it?
- If you don't have a mission statement, would you like to create one?
- What will you include?
- What breathes within you for release?

- Who are you - really?
- If you have a mission statement, what is in it? Do you remember?

Patience

Patience

Does practice make perfect?

Imagine for a moment that you are walking in a garden. This garden is perfect in every way. There is a winding path, plenty of lush green vegetation, and a cornucopia of delicious flowers. The garden takes your breath away. You could stay there forever, just breathing it all in.

And then you remember. This is not *your* garden. Your garden is full of weeds that you've pulled that have suddenly but not surprisingly managed to grow back. It is full of plants that need watering and roots that need digging, and plenty of tending through the seasons.

No, this is not *your* garden.

Celeste

Patience… some possess it as a gift, natural and a way of being. Others, draw upon it easily. Some, like me, can find this attribute allusive at best.

Impatience, in the way I view life, can be synonymous with a need for perfection, or rather, imposing my perfectionistic ways on others. Beware, both impatience and perfection may seduce you into regretful activities. Impatience is often fueled by other emotions.

1987, Fort Riley Kansas. Chris' last duty station before separating from the U.S. Army. Chris, myself, and our 3½ year old son Aaron, were living in a singlewide mobile home in Ogden KS. Ever been in Kansas in spring and summer? Hot, humid, sticky weather, magnificent yet often scary storms, beautiful country side, amazing people, mesmerizing fireflies.

On this particular hot, humid day, way too hot for a young boy to stay inside, Aaron had been out playing with friends, doing whatever little boys do on such a day. Dad was at work and I was busy doing what mom's did then, inside trying to figure out how to stay cool in 98 degree 90 percent humidity weather without air conditioning!

After some time out playing, Aaron returned. He was a happy little guy, gentle and easy going by nature. Tender hearted. He had had a full day of fun and now needed some rest from the day's activities. I do not recall all the details of the events that transpired on his return but I do have painful recall of this event…

He had returned barefoot, without shoes in hand. When I queried as to where he had left his shoes he simply replied, "I don't know." And with those words it began, my impatience.

"What do you mean, you don't know? How could you not know where you took your shoes off?"

Again in his innocent little 3½ year old voice: "I don't know."

My voice now rising and becoming stern: "Aaron, where did you leave your shoes?'

Aaron's tiny voice now sheepish and almost fearful: "I don't know."

My voice now taken over by out of control emotions, anger, panic, fear (after all how would I be able to replace those shoes, we were living on such a tight budget. Didn't Aaron at 3 ½ years old understand all of this?): "You go out there right now and find your shoes and don't come back in until you do!

As his big blue eyes became sad and his head bent down I felt it…

A 3½ year old boy's heart breaking. Breaking because mother; his caregiver, nurturer, protector, defender, had lost control of her emotions and turned against that tiny heart!

Mother had become impatient.

Impatience is not an attribute synonymous with "mother".

I could not feel the depth of pain in his heart but I could see it. In that moment my heart, too, broke. How could I have done such a thing? How could I have been so emotionally out of control to have caused such damage?

Well, many years later, very recently actually in contemplation of adding this "glimpse" to this book, I spoke with Aaron about this event as I asked for his permission to tell this story. He does not remember this happening, yet, I recall it, not the details, but the painful heart because I carried it all these years. Aaron is now 32 years old.

Patience is a gift of charity. Charity is a gift from Heavenly Father. Some possess the gift, some easily draw on it, yet others must seek for it and ask for the gift.

Impatience is a weed. One to be ever aware of as it can so easily choke out the beauty in our lives, our relationships.

I continue to ask. I continue to "practice" and make "progress", hoping to one day be made perfect. Herein lies Heaven 24/7. How else can we obtain this gift but through the atonement. As I ask for this gift and with each event that occurs through which I may practice patience, Heaven meets out another portion.

Kathryn

Planting a tree is easy. Waiting for it to grow takes patience. Perhaps that is why I love trees so much. If I plant the tree deep enough, and continue to nurture and take care of it, the tree will grow. When it is old enough, perhaps so old that I am no longer on this earth, it might be cut down, it may become a stump, and even then it will serve.

The idea of growing and, at the same time, taking care of others, whether that care is shade, precious fruit, or a nice place to sit, fills me with joy.

And I want to be like that.

Still, it is not always easy to serve.

Sometimes, I feel as if I'm being taken for a ride, or I feel as if I'm a doormat, taking in the words someone is dishing out, or experiencing the parts they are playing in their life as if they are my own.

We are to have genuine sympathy for others, but should we also be taking on someone else's very burden? Isn't there someone else for that?

I remember the day I sighed a great sigh of relief because my children were all grown and had moved away. I couldn't believe it. I was finally an empty nester! I'd looked forward to this day for years. In my mind I'd already planned great vacations with my husband, and moments alone, oh, those moments alone, where, undisturbed, we'd share with each other the desires of our hearts.

Okay, so it was a dream.

Six months later, after our youngest girl had moved out, our middle daughter and her son moved in. She was pregnant with her second child. Talk was, divorce.

We lived in a two bedroom condo on the fourth floor. My daughter and her son shared the room that had been vacated by my youngest daughter. Within weeks a basinet sat scrunched in one corner. How would we all fit when the baby came in one month?

We had to move, but we waited until the time was right.

Six months later a rental opened up, and because our lease was up at just that time, too, we were able to move. We shared this living space for four years, and although the space was greater than what we'd just left, and more conducive to children, the time together was still difficult.

At the end of four years we decided to move once again. This time we bought a house with an almost finished basement. And you can probably guess what happened next. My daughter and her children made an apartment downstairs, and my husband and I shared the top floor - though the kitchen and laundry room were used by the both of us.

And we are still here.

If patience is a virtue, I must be a tree.

I keep asking myself, *"What's up with the repeat course in raising children?" "How many more years will I need to share my kitchen and laundry room with my daughter?" "How many more years before I go completely mad, or she finishes school?"*

But maybe, just maybe I am asking myself the wrong questions.

Like a tree whose leaves change with the seasons and fall off, only to be nourished again by the good will of God and the hands of his children, I am the same. I am growing. I am changing. And maybe, just maybe, the Lord in his infinite mercy is teaching me how to grow.

- Are you progressing?
- Or, are you expecting yourself and others to go straight to perfect?
- Are you living Heaven 24/7 by learning of and applying the atonement?

Mercy

Mercy

Are you ready for a heart change?

Imagine for a moment that your heart can be weighed, and that this weighing on the scale of life has something else on the other side -- a feather. The truth will soon be revealed. What will this truth be? Will your heart weigh more than the feather or the feather more than your heart?

Looking at this scene realistically, it's quite obvious in your mind what will weigh the most. But what if you were told that the feather had to weigh more than your heart for you to pass on to the next life? What if the *feather* had to be heavier?

"Well, that's impossible. A feather can never be heavier than a heart, it's a proven fact." But what if it could? What would it take? Or more pointedly, *who* would it take? You'd need a miracle, right? Someone who could make a feather heavier than a heart.

With all of our doings, all of our learning, all of what we try to improve upon, even with all of our being, there is only one who can tip the scales for us, and that person is Christ.

Kathryn

I haven't always understood the gift of mercy. It was just easier to pass judgment rather than go to a place that always made me feel like a doormat.

But I had it all wrong - all of it.

Mercy, those tender mercies that the Lord gives us are heartfelt. Because the Lord's heart has already been changed, he can give us the tender mercy that we need from him.

What about us?

A few weeks ago as I sat with a friend, struggling with how to overcome this weakness within me, I just couldn't see how giving mercy was possible. I just couldn't see how I might ever get there knowing the inconsistencies of everyone and the terrible weaknesses within myself.

How could I really ever truly be merciful without faking it?

That very day, the word mercy whirled within my head like an air conditioned unit. I thought about it over and over, wondering how I could be different, how I could finally, once and for all, give mercy to others - without holding back, without saying what I wasn't feeling, without being - fake.

And then it came, believe it or not, in the form of a British television program - *Doctor Who* no less. If you haven't seen *Doctor Who*, a time-travel, monster laden, science fiction futuristic sort of drama, then you've been missing out. Truly.

During this particular episode, the Doctor travels back in time to see a little boy who will die if he doesn't save him. The little boy is calling out, "Help me, save me," and the Doctor is hesitating. Why? Because he also knows this little boy in the future, and this little boy, now some sort of mechanical man, has turned his back on goodness. He has chosen wickedness.

What does the Doctor do, knowing what he knows?

Does he let the little child die, knowing what he will one day become?

Will he save him, because he is the Doctor, and the Doctor has compassion?

In truth, we already know what the Doctor does, because the mechanical man is still alive. The Doctor has chosen to save the child.

It is up to us to give mercy even when the other person doesn't deserve it. When they might be cruel to us, when they might not think they've done anything wrong. If we see each individual as the child of God they are, if we allow God to change our heavy and hardened heart, we have no room for judgment. None.

Celeste

Mercy, forgiveness from heaven. Mercy, comfort from heaven, Mercy, relief extended by heaven. Mercy, guidance by heaven. Mercy, protection from heaven. Mercy, healing balm of heaven, This is only a small list of the effects of mercy that I have received in my life.

Two of my most cherished hymns invoke strong and tender emotions when I think of or sing their words:..."streams of mercy never ceasing, call for songs of loudest praise", and ..."come to the mercy seat, fervently kneel." I reflect on the exquisite mercy seat spoken of in Exodus, the place where God's glory rested as he met with His people, and the Throne of God in other Old Testament writings. How is it that I, as such an imperfect being, am invited to the mercy seat?

When I have fallen, I have been picked up. When I have erred, I have been corrected., When I have sinned, I have been forgiven. When I have been angry, I have been chastened and humbled. When I have been wounded, I have been consoled and comforted. When I... It has not mattered the circumstance, mercy has been extended.

So, back to my question: How is it that I, as such an imperfect being, am invited to the mercy seat? For me, it is by the immeasurable love and grace of my Father and the Savior. Nothing short of that. Miraculous, yes. An attribute that I seek, yes. One, akin to charity, that I pray I can receive as a heavenly gift.

In my human state, extending mercy can be quite challenging. It takes work on my part. I must be willing to approach the mercy seat. I must be willing to set aside my pride. I must be willing to repent and ask for forgiveness first. I must see the other person as a child of God in the flesh. Just as prone to error as I am, they are no less than I. I must ask for a greater capacity to love and the ability to extend that love.

Mercy does not require that I understand the person or circumstance. To me, that is judgment. Unlike the judgments I must make daily to keep safe to make correct decisions, the judgments involved with mercy can only be correctly made by Heavenly Father and the Savior. For me, needing understanding can be a trap that keeps me tied to my pride.

This is what I know; the streams of mercy are constant, unwavering. The streams of mercy are never ceasing. This is what this whole book is about! Daily, moment to moment, they are evident throughout my life.

And so I sing songs of loudest praise!

- Do you have room for mercy?
- Is your hardened heart, softened?
- Would you like it to be?

Love

Love

Might it look different than you think?

It's the end of your journey, and you are worried. *What will he think?* you wonder. *What will he - ask? What will he say?*

As you walk up the path that has only been played out in your mind's eye until now, you wonder about these questions and more. Are you ready? Are you clean? Did you do all that was required of you while on the earth? Did you repent of all your sins? Did you seek him as you promised?

At the end of the lane you see him. But you are sure he has seen you first. His arms are outstretched and he is smiling.

So, this is it, you are thinking. There's no going back. Only forward. There he is. Just steps away now. You see his eyes. They are a vivid blue, just as you imagined them to be.

He takes you in his arms. You wait, the joy of his embrace making you feel whole - complete. This is joy like you've only felt in short bursts before, not like this. You feel warm. You feel happy. You feel loved.

"Welcome home," God says.

Kathryn

I watched a show on life after death recently with my husband. Although I'd heard many of the concepts of dying before - the tunnel, the bright light, family members waiting to receive you - there was a constant mention from almost everyone about something else - the only thing they could really take with them.

People said this heavenly love was almost in-explainable. They felt more love wrapped around them during their experience in heaven, than they believed was humanly possible. Everyone exuded this love. Everyone. And love was all there was.

Imagine that. Love. Just love. Not worrying about what errands they had to do or the hurt they were feeling or even what to make for dinner. Just love on a glorious, never-to-be forgotten plate.

Imagine.

Living heaven 24/7 is a little bit like that, and a little bit not like that. For with any dream, any wish, any desire for change, there needs to be something just as important, and that thing is action.

Action can be pretty scary. It can feel overwhelming, like scaling Mount Everest.

But love in its truest and brightest sense, accomplishes all things.

Celeste

A few years ago our daughter, Chelsea, began the transition from teen-hood to adulthood and moved out of our home and into her own apartment with her cousin as her roommate. This was a great arrangement for quite some time, though the day did come that the arrangement would change. Her cousin was getting married. Chelsea would now have the responsibility of the apartment all to herself.

As most parents would do, Chris and I basically went into "stopgap" mode. We offered Chelsea the option of moving back home until she found another place to live as her apartment was not necessarily inexpensive. She was making good money but we were not sure her single income would be sufficient. She assured us though that she would be fine and all would work out okay.

Chris and I relaxed on the subject and life went on.

Late one evening, 9:30-10:00 o'clockish, through the miracle of technology, a text to my phone delivered a long, unnerving message. The short version was: "Mom, Jason (Chelsea's long time beau since high school) and I are going to live together. We know you will be disappointed but it's what we want." I was Stunned.

I walked to Chris' office, stared at him for a moment, and handed him my phone. He read the message. He stared at me for a moment.
Emotions raced but we stayed in control.

We knew immediate action was necessary.
Technology delivered our message back: We'd like to come and see you.

Chelsea's response: I'm scared to but okay.

Not a lot of words were shared on the drive over to the apartment. Many thoughts. Really, what do you do when your adult child makes a decision that you not only don't agree with but flies in the face of what you have strived to teach them their whole life?

Pray, be still, listen.

Things were awkward but not tense as we sat down together. The conversation tender. Chris and I knew that the kids had made their decision and it was theirs to make, not ours. And yet, we remained Chelsea's parents. What were we to do? A strong sense of "continue to teach, admonish, warn-with love" came over me.

It was time.

In a flash my personal life experiences flowed through me. I knew it was time to share many details of my life with my daughter; things she would never have imagined would have taken place in her mother's life. As they flowed through me they flowed out to her. Powerful experiences that bore witness to the possible consequences of her decision. Nothing was spared or hidden. She had chosen a path, a path I once knew and had turned from. There could be no "but you don't understand" or "why didn't you tell me", because I "did" on both counts.

And so, Chris and I taught, admonished, warned, and loved as we'd been instructed.

Still, after the visit, we remained unsettled.

We decided to go and counsel with our clergy, just to have a listening ear to talk through things with. It was here that a marvelous lesson and miracle came.

In the course of our conversation, we were asked what we felt toward the kids. Our immediate response, almost in perfect unity, was "we love them both!"

"Then be happy!" came this response from our counselor.

Be happy…with those words came the miracle. All unsettled feelings, all sting from the situation, any sadness left my heart. Challenging feelings were replaced with joy and hope and a deepened love toward our children.

You see, we were taught these fundamental and eternal principles: We are not our children's first parents. They first have Heavenly parents. We have been given the privilege to bear them here, raise and teach them (which we have done) but we have not been given the right to judge them. That right belongs to their Heavenly parents only. We have not been given the right to take away their agency. That has belonged to them throughout the eternities. We have been charged with the right and privilege to LOVE them. Love is the greatest commandment….

Chris and I continue to pray, teach, admonish, and warn. We are parents. As a family, Chris and I, Aaron, Chelsea, and Jason, are strong together. Our love toward one another continues to grow. We are so richly blessed!

Every choice we are given to make is direct evidence of our connection to Heaven 24/7. Chelsea and Jason could have made a different choice and may still. Chris and I could have made a different choice and damaged or even lost our relationship with our children. With each choice we face, we have power to block the receiving of blessings from Heaven or stay in the flow of Heaven which is constantly around us and have our blessings added upon.

Love is a choice.

- When have you chosen to love? Was it easy?
- What did you learn about yourself because you chose it?
- What did you learn about the other person because you chose to love?
- Are you choosing to be in the flow of Heaven 24/7 even if it looks different than you think it ought to? If not, are you willing to start today?

Epilogue

Epilogue

Did you see them? The "Glimpses" of your life? Did they stir in you? Did they come to your recall? Did you begin to write them? Oh, how we hope that you did. For you see, you too live Heaven 24/7.

At times you may see dimly, have a tub that needs cleaning, forget that you are the gardener, have stones to give away, feel small, have tough choices to make to show mercy and love, etc… yes, these experiences will happen in this part of eternity called mortal life.

Kathryn and I hope that you see each of your personal "Glimpses" as the unique events that they are. Designed just for you. For your experience and growth. You too, are now, always have been, and always will be, connected to Heaven 24/7, connected to the Light. May you forever seek and choose to see clearly through the Light.

Next?

Do you have a story to share? We'd love to see it! We are looking for true stories on faith, courage, repentance, growth, fear, hope, joy, love and more.

What has occurred in your life that has changed you - made you better for having experienced it? When have you felt as if heaven was surrounding you? Have you heard angels sing? Have you felt as if you were in the presence of God? Have you been changed?

Submit your story of under 1,000 words at: www.heaven24-7.com.

We may use it for out next book, and if we do, we'll send you a free copy and direct access to ordering additional books at a discount!

We would LOVE for you to be a part of Heaven 24/7.

Kathryn Elizabeth Jones

KATHRYN has been a published writer since 1987. She started as a newspaper reporter, published her first novel in 2002, attended college in her 40s, and opened the doors to Idea Creations Press in 2012. She has published eight books to date in the genres of Christian fiction, mystery, nonfiction (including Christian and business) and one middle reader. Kathryn offers opportunities for authors to get their books out there using her publishing services.

You can contact Kathryn at:

kathy@ariverofstones.com

kathryn@heaven24-7.com

www.ideacreationspress.com

M. Celeste Martin

CELESTE was born and raised on the beautiful Monterey Bay in California. She has been married to her sweetheart, Chris, for 32 years. She is the mother of 2 amazing children, Aaron and Chelsea. Her educational background is in Speech Communication and Public Speaking. She currently works full time and is a business entrepreneur and mentor. Through mentoring she works to help others see that they are not "broken".

One of her greatest loves and gifts is singing. To her, singing is a language that literally keeps her connected to heaven 24/7.

You can contact Celeste at:
mylife@martinlegacy.net.
celeste@heaven24-7.com